RE in the Classroom

with 4-5s

50 easy-to-use Bible-based lesson plans for teaching essential life skills

Helen Jaeger

Text copyright © Helen Jaeger 2015
The author asserts the moral right
to be identified as the author of this work

Published by
The Bible Reading Fellowship
15 The Chambers, Vineyard
Abingdon OX14 3FE
United Kingdom
Tel: +44 (0)1865 319700
Email: enquiries@brf.org.uk
Website: www.brf.org.uk
BRF is a Registered Charity

ISBN 978 1 84101 614 6

First published 2015
10 9 8 7 6 5 4 3 2 1 0

Cover photo: © monkeybusinessimages/iStock/Thinkstock

A catalogue record for this book is available from the British Library

Printed by Gutenberg Press, Tarxien, Malta

Important information

Photocopying permission

The right to photocopy material in *RE in the Classroom with 4–5s* is granted for the pages that contain the photocopying clause: 'Reproduced with permission from *RE in the Classroom with 4–5s* by Helen Jaeger (Barnabas in Schools, 2015) www.barnabasinschools.org.uk', so long as reproduction is for use in a teaching situation by the original purchaser. The right to photocopy material is not granted for anyone other than the original purchaser without written permission from BRF.

The Copyright Licensing Agency (CLA)

If you are resident in the UK and you have a photocopying licence with the Copyright Licensing Agency (CLA) please check the terms of your licence. If your photocopying request falls within the terms of your licence, you may proceed without seeking further permission. If your request exceeds the terms of your CLA licence, please contact the CLA directly with your request. Copyright Licensing Agency, Saffron House, 6–10 Kirby Street, London EC1N 8TS. Telephone 020 7400 3100; fax 020 7400 3101; email cla@cla.co.uk; web www.cla.co.uk. The CLA will provide photocopying authorisation and royalty fee information on behalf of BRF.

BRF is a Registered Charity (No. 233280)

To Jan,

with thanks for your

encouragement and support

Contents

Classroom sessions

Introduction

This book has been designed for you to pick up and use straight away. The material covers key learning areas for the 4–5s age group, such as playing fairly, developing independence, eating healthily, making friends and following rules. Through it, you will be able to address the RE and Personal, Social and Health needs of your class or group.

Department for Education (DfE) emphases include security, safety, happiness, ability and talents for all children. Early Years Foundation Stage (EYFS) is about providing a 'good foundation for future progress through school and life' (DfE). Other key areas to note include encouraging children to be resilient, capable, confident, self-assured, strong, independent, responsive and positive. Listening, understanding and learning are natural cornerstones of the curriculum.

The 50 lesson plans in this resource offer fun and interactive ways to explore these themes. Activities are practical, creative and inclusive. The lesson plans are listed alphabetically for ease of reference, following a format of:

- game or activity
- questions
- discussion
- Bible story
- reflection

You may like to combine sessions for a themed day or week or for assemblies. See the Sloth's story in the Appendix (page 61) for an example.

I hope you find this book accessible and useful, and that you enjoy leading and supporting your children as they grow and learn.

How to look up a Bible reference

Throughout this resource, you will find references to stories and events from the Bible. If you're not familiar with it, the Christian Bible is a collection of different books, each with its own name—for example, Genesis or Matthew. The books are divided into numbered chapters and further subdivided into numbered verses.

In this resource, you will find Bible references shown in the following format: **Matthew 12:1–6**. In this case, Matthew is the name of the book, 12 is the chapter number and 1–6 is the sequence of verses to be read within that chapter.

If you need to read more than one chapter of a book (for example, Exodus chapters 7 to 12), it will be shown in the following format: **Exodus 7—12**.

If you want to read the story directly from the Bible, you will find a list of the books in order at the beginning of any Bible. Turn to the book that you want and find the chapter, then the verses. You can also look up references online at www.biblegateway.com or by typing the Bible reference directly into your usual search engine.

How to encourage answers and discussion

There are lots of opportunities for discussion sessions in this book, which encourage your children to interact and learn. As you will know, children of this age are often creative and enthusiastic. They are growing in imagination, curiosity and ideas. They like to try out new things, including ideas. They are becoming more able at weighing up different choices and even the quietest children show a keen interest in the world around them. Many are developing social skills, building friendships and figuring out what they do and don't like.

- Allow for a wide range of expression according to personality, but make sure that everyone in your group feels they are a valued member with something to contribute. In particular, look for ways to encourage and praise quieter members, who might otherwise be overshadowed by their more extravert peers in question-and-answer discussions.

- Coach children in how to work out a problem, by asking open-ended questions and building on the discussion from the children themselves.

- Offer praise and encouragement. Children thrive in a positive environment where they feel that their ideas (and those of others), however tentative, will be received and encouraged.

- Look for a variety of ways to praise for ideas, skill, creativity and participation.

- Offer support and 'nudges' but don't take over. Let children explore and try out new things for themselves under your guidance.

- Let them choose. Children love to have a go at choosing and expressing themselves. Encourage this in their answers and ideas, asking leading and open questions.

- Help them to finish what they start: children enjoy completing a project or game. Allow sufficient time in your sessions or add more time in a different session if you need to.

- Encourage focus and structure. If you feel that a session or discussion is moving off-topic, gently steer it back. Children generally like structure and feel safe within it.

- Allow collaboration and discussion within peer groups. Some children like to learn by looking at how others are doing things and absorb information more passively.

- Allow unusual ideas. Even something that doesn't work can become a lesson in discussing why it didn't work. This also encourages a positive 'I can try' attitude without fear of criticism or ridicule.

- Allow time for reflection and summing up. Some children get lost in an over-general discussion and appreciate a summary from a person they trust.

- Include everyone within your discussions and ensure that all members of your group feel they have had a chance to express themselves, listen, learn and contribute.

Of course, every child is unique and learns at a different pace. Creating a safe, open and stimulating place for them to explore issues is rewarding both for you and the children.

Bible story summary chart

Theme	Bible story	Bible reference
Asking for help	Moses, the leader, is doing too much and getting confused. Someone suggests that he gets some help.	Exodus 18:13–24
Assertiveness	A blind man wants Jesus to heal him. The crowd tell him to be quiet, but he ignores them and asks Jesus anyway.	Luke 18:35–43
Beautiful world	God makes the world and everything in it.	Genesis 1
Being careful	Jesus meets a deaf man who wants Jesus to heal him. The place is crowded with people. Jesus takes him to a quiet place to heal him.	Mark 7:31–37
Being forgiving	One of Jesus' best friends, Peter, asks him how many times he should forgive someone if they have done something wrong. Jesus gives Peter a surprising answer.	Matthew 18:21–35
Our bodies	King David writes a poem about how amazing our bodies are and how amazing God is.	Psalm 139:13–18
Cared for	Jesus tells people not to worry, because God cares about even the tiniest details of their lives.	Luke 12:22–29
Celebrations	Jesus tells a story about a king who throws a party.	Matthew 22:1–10
Confidence	An unknown Christian writer tells some other Christians that God loves them and they can be confident about asking God for help.	Hebrews 4:16
Creativity	God made the whole world. Imagine how creative God is!	Genesis 2:19–20
Curiosity	A short man called Zacchaeus wants to see Jesus, so he climbs a tree to get a better look.	Luke 19:1–6
Eating	Jesus feeds 5000 people.	Luke 9:12–17
Fairness	Jesus tells a story about a man who has two sons.	Luke 15:11–32
Family	God tells Noah and his family to build an ark to save themselves from a flood.	Genesis 6:9 — 7:10
Fear	God wants to protect people, especially when they feel scared.	Psalm 28:7
Friends	Jesus chooses twelve people to be his special friends.	Matthew 4:18–22
Fun	Jesus is at a wedding and everyone is having fun. When they run out of wine, he makes more for them.	John 2:1–11
Generosity	Jesus tells people that God is generous because he provides for good and bad people.	Matthew 5:43–48
Growing	Jesus grows up in his family.	Luke 2:51–52
Guidance	The Israelites need to cross the desert. God gives them special signs to guide them.	Exodus 13:20–22
Happiness	James writes a letter to his friends and tells them what to do when they are happy.	James 5:13
Health	King Hezekiah is very ill and prays to God, asking God to make him well again. God listens.	Isaiah 38:1–8
Independence	God tells Abraham to leave his country and relatives and promises to bless him.	Genesis 12:1–4
Kindness	Jesus tells a story about a man who gets beaten up. A kind stranger finds him and helps him to get better.	Luke 10:30–37
Learning	Paul writes a letter to his friend Timothy, telling him that the Bible helps people to learn how to live well.	2 Timothy 3:14–17
Loyalty	David had a best friend called Jonathan. When David becomes king, he looks after Jonathan's family, too.	2 Samuel 9

Making mistakes	One of Jesus' best friends, Peter, lets him down, but Jesus knows that Peter made a mistake and they become friends again.	John 21:4–17
Making things	King Solomon builds a very special temple for the worship of God.	1 Kings 6 and 7
Moving	God hears the cries of his people and decides it's time to help them move away from Egypt. But does Pharaoh agree?	Exodus 7 – 12
Obedience	Moses advises the people to be obedient to God so that things will go well for them.	Deuteronomy 30:11–16
Patience	Jesus' friends go fishing but catch nothing. Jesus tells them to have one last go.	John 21:1–6
Paying attention	God talks to a boy called Samuel.	1 Samuel 3:1–10
Peace	Jesus appears to his friends and tells them not to be afraid.	John 20:19–21
Playing	Jesus says that he likes children and wants them to come to him.	Matthew 19:13–15
Presents	An angel visits Mary and brings her good news about a special baby.	Luke 1:26–38
Respect	Daniel loves God and always puts him first, above everything else. God protects Daniel, even in a lion's den.	Daniel 6:1–23
Rest	When God finishes making the world, he has a rest.	Genesis 2:1–4
Rules	God gives Moses the ten commandments to help the people live well together.	Exodus 20:1–17
Safety	Three wise men visit the baby Jesus, but King Herod wants to kill the baby. God warns them in a dream to avoid Herod.	Matthew 2:1–12
Security	Jesus tells a story about foolish and wise builders.	Matthew 7:24–29
Sharing	Ruth follows her mother-in-law, Naomi, to a new country.	Ruth 1:1–18
Specialness	Jesus tells a story about a sheep getting lost.	Luke 15:3–7
Sticking up for others	Mary and Martha have a brother called Lazarus, who is very ill. They ask Jesus to come and make him better.	John 11:1–44
Stories	Jesus teaches from a boat.	Mark 4:1–32
Talents	Jesus tells a story about three people who each have different talents.	Matthew 25:14–30
Teaching	Jesus teaches his friends how to pray and answers their question.	Luke 11:1–4
Truth	Jesus asks his friends who people say he really is.	Luke 9:18–20
Unique	Jesus walks on the water of a lake.	John 6:16–21
Watching	Joshua sends two spies into Jericho.	Joshua 2:1–15
Working together	God rewards people who have worked well together to make the world a better place for everyone.	Matthew 25:31–40

Asking for help

Starter activity: Dress up!

Divide the class into equal-sized teams. Give each team an assortment of dressing-up items: scarf, gloves, hat, button-up coat and a novelty item such as fake glasses or a wig. Seat each team in a circle.

Explain that the game starts with one person sitting in the middle of each circle. When you give the signal, that person must get dressed. They can only get dressed by asking for help—with no words, just pointing or gesturing—and the rest of the team must dress them. Once that person is dressed, they take off the dressing-up clothes and the next person has a go, until everyone in the team has had a turn. The winning team is the one that finishes first.

Warn the team that you will make them do it again if you spot anyone talking or doing it without help.

Ask...

What would it be like if everyone in the world helped everyone else?

Discuss...

How can we be more helpful to each other? Do you think it would be nice to become a classroom of helpers?

> **Examples:** sharing things together; helping someone who is lost; saving a seat for someone; answering a question if you know the answer; letting someone borrow a pencil; helping with special jobs, such as showing people where to put things away.

What the Bible says: Exodus 18:13–24

Story: Help! Moses is doing too much

Moses was in charge of a very large group of people. He was a bit like a head teacher in charge of a school. But he was the only one doing the work. An older member of his family, called Jethro, watched Moses at work. He was worried that Moses was doing too much and that he would get tired. Jethro said he thought God cared, too. He told Moses he should get other people to help him. Moses thought this was a good idea and he tried it out. It turned out that Jethro was right. After Moses asked for help, everything went a lot better.

What can we learn from the story?

Even though Moses was a wise leader, he needed help. His father-in-law saw that and helped Moses to realise it. By accepting someone else's help, Moses learnt something and became better at what he was doing.

Reflection

Doing things by ourselves—learning to tie our shoelaces or going to the toilet at break time—is a good thing, but we all need help at times. Maybe it's with a problem, like a maths sum you can't solve or a word you don't know how to spell. Or maybe you are worried about something or a friend is unhappy. Instead of trying to solve the problem by yourself, it can be good to ask for help.

Assertiveness

Starter activity: 'What if?'

Devise a range of scenarios your children might face, in which they need to be assertive. Examples could include, if someone said:

- you couldn't join in their game.
- you couldn't stand next to them in the lunch queue.
- you couldn't ask the teacher for help.
- you'd done something naughty when you hadn't.
- you couldn't sit at their table.
- you couldn't be friends with someone else.
- your idea was silly.

Using a stuffed toy, explain that your toy is shy and needs help to get himself heard. What advice would the children give to your toy for each of the above situations? Act them out, perhaps using other puppets or toys as well.

Ask...

Can you think of situations in which it might be good to ask for something that you need or want? How can you ask politely and get what you need?

> **Examples:** if someone is being nasty to you and you need to let someone know about it; if someone is being unfair to you; if you need help with something; if you want to help someone else; if someone else has done something naughty and is blaming you; if you need something like pens or pencils.

Discuss...

What would it be like if some people got their own way all the time? Why is it important that everyone gets heard?

What the Bible says: Luke 18:35–43

Story: A blind man asks Jesus to heal him

There was a blind man living in a city called Jericho. He would sit by the side of the road, begging for food and money. One day he heard a large crowd going past. He asked what was happening. The crowd told him Jesus was going by. The blind man knew that Jesus could do special things, like making blind people see. When he heard that Jesus was nearby, he called out to him. The crowd near the blind man told him to be quiet, but the blind man ignored them and shouted even louder.

Jesus heard the man and asked his friends to bring him over. When the blind man was in front of him, Jesus asked him what he wanted. The blind man told Jesus he wanted to see. Jesus agreed and made him better.

What can we learn from the story?

The blind man never gives up. First he wants to know what all the noise is about. Then he shouts out to Jesus. And when Jesus asks him what he wants, he's not afraid to say. He speaks up for himself and asks for something good.

Reflection

Sometimes it is good to ask for what we want or need. Even if other people tell us to be quiet, it can be good to keep on asking, especially when you're asking for something you really need or for someone else.

Beautiful world

Starter activity: Nature sense

Explain that you're going on a nature walk. (It could be a walk in the school playground or an excursion to a local park or nature reserve.) You're going to use all your senses.

To start, stand the group in a circle. Ask everyone to close their eyes and listen. Each time someone hears a new noise from nature—a bird singing or the leaves of a tree rustling—they should put their hand up. How many things can they hear?

Now, ask everyone to stand in one spot and look all around. What can they see? Make a list. Next, spend a few minutes smelling the air, or a tree, or the grass. What does it smell like? Write a describing sentence.

See if your group can find everything on a 'treasure list' (it can be fun to use cheap magnifying glasses for the smaller items). For example, they might look for something that is:

- furry
- orange
- growing
- rough
- smooth
- tall
- tiny
- black
- slimy
- dry
- silver
- the size of their hand
- thin
- crunchy
- a leaf
- a seed
- a rock
- soil
- grass
- a twig

Make a hand-drawn map, listing everything you discovered.

Ask...

Were you surprised by anything you heard, saw and touched? How much variety was there? What did you think was the most beautiful?

Discuss...

What is your favourite thing in nature? Why? What can you do to look after it?

> **Examples:** not leaving litter around; feeding family pets; watering plants or seeds; keeping your eyes and ears open for nature whenever you go on a walk.

What the Bible says: Genesis 1

Story: God makes the world

The Bible begins with a story of God creating the world. God creates everything in order, starting with light and darkness, night and day. Next comes the sky, then the sea and continents; after that come plants and trees and other green things. Then God makes stars, the sun and the moon, then sea creatures and birds; after that, animals and insects; and finally human beings. God is really happy with all of creation and blesses it.

What can we learn from the story?

God loves the world—from aardvarks and ants to yaks and zebras, and everything in between. The world is an amazing place, full of variety, not just in animals but in plants and even the stars and the seas, countries and human beings.

Reflection

The world is full of beauty and we have an important role to play in looking after it. Everyone can do something simple to look after our beautiful world.

Being careful

Starter activity: Egg and spoon race

Explain that you're going to play an egg and spoon race. Divide the class into teams and give each team a teaspoon and a hard-boiled egg (or similar). Now the teams race against each other without dropping the egg from the spoon. Any person who drops the egg has to go back to the starting line and run again. The team that wins is the one in which every member has reached the finishing line, complete with egg and spoon.

Ask...

What would it be like if we didn't care for anything—if we treated things roughly or without care?

> **Example:** things would break and we wouldn't be able to use them any more.

Discuss...

Why is it important to treat things with respect? What sorts of things do we need to be careful with? What happens if we don't treat people carefully, too? Would it be nice to be in a class where you felt that everyone was going to treat you well?

> **Examples:** personal belongings; items at home such as cups and plates; we need to treat each other with respect—people can get sad or have hurt feelings.

What the Bible says: Mark 7:31–37

Story: Jesus is considerate to a deaf man

One day some people brought a deaf man to Jesus. They asked him to help him and heal him. There were lots of people there, so Jesus took the man away from the crowds. He touched the deaf man gently and prayed a special prayer. As soon as he'd prayed, the man could hear and speak. Everyone was amazed.

What can we learn from the story?

Jesus wanted to show the deaf man that he cared about him. He treated him carefully, with politeness and courtesy. Jesus was concerned for the deaf man's feelings as well as for his physical needs.

Reflection

Sometimes it's important to think about how other people are feeling and try not to make them feel embarrassed. We should be careful with other people and their feelings, not just with things. It's nice when people care for us in this way and when we care about them, too.

Being forgiving

Starter activity: Scribble erase

Ask the children to list things that are naughty, such as 'fighting with my brother or sister', 'being rude', 'not telling the truth', 'not doing what my mum asks', 'going to bed late' and so on. Scribble the ideas on to a whiteboard. Now take a whiteboard eraser and rub it all out, until the board is really clear and clean. Explain that forgiveness is like the eraser: it wipes out everything naughty that we've done.

Ask...

What would it be like if your mum or dad remembered all the naughty things you had ever done and reminded you of them every time you did something else naughty?

Discuss...

What is forgiveness? Is it always right to forgive someone? To forgive someone means not to bring up the past things they've done wrong. Is that a good thing?

What the Bible says: Matthew 18:21–35

Story: Jesus talks about forgiveness

One of Jesus' best friends was a man called Peter. One day Peter came to Jesus and asked him, 'How many times must I forgive someone who does something wrong against me?'

Jesus told Peter a story. Jesus said that there was a servant who owed the king lots of money. He couldn't pay it back, so he decided he would beg the king to let him off. He fell at the king's feet and said, 'I can't pay all this money back. Please let me off!' The king felt sorry for the man and let him off. But as soon as that man left the king, he bumped into another servant, who owed him money. He grabbed the servant by the neck and demanded he pay it back. The servant wasn't able to, so the man threw him into prison.

Other servants were upset about what happened and told the king all about it. He was furious! He'd let this man off, but the man hadn't treated the other servant the same way. So the king summoned the bad servant and threw him in prison until he'd paid back every penny he owed.

What can we learn from the story?

Christians believe that God is like a king who wants to let people off their faults and debts. God treats people kindly and generously. God wants people to be generous to other people, too. Jesus said we should forgive because God forgives us.

Reflection

Forgiving other people when they do something silly is a good thing to do, because we all do silly things. Of course, if someone does something really wrong that hurts someone, it's good to tell a teacher or someone else who can help.

Bodies

Starter activity: 'Heads and shoulders' song

Sing 'Heads, shoulders, knees and toes'. Point to each part of the body as you sing the song. (If you're not sure of the tune or words, have a look online.) Extend the song by leaving out words as you sing, until you are pointing to all the parts of your body without words. Speed up as you sing.

Ask...

What do you like most about your body? What amazing things is your body able to do?

Discuss...

Your body is amazing! How can you look after it properly?

> **Examples:** washing your hands; cleaning your teeth; getting help with any cuts or bruises; getting enough sleep; enjoying using your body's strengths by jumping, skipping, running or swimming.

What the Bible says: Psalm 139:13–18

Story: King David writes a poem about the body

King David wrote many poems. In one poem, he said that the human body is amazing and that God created it. He said that God 'knitted' him together when he was just a tiny baby growing inside his mother. He said the human body is wonderful and that everything God makes is wonderful. King David believed that because God had made him, God knew him very well and cared about him very much.

What can we learn from the story?

King David believed that God is good and loving and that God made human beings to be amazing, too. He didn't mean to say how great he was, in a proud way, but because he realised that our bodies are amazing creations.

Reflection

God cares about everything in our lives, even the tiny details, like the colour of our eyes or how high we can jump. God loves us very much and made our bodies for us to enjoy and to look after.

Cared for

Starter activity: Ravens and flowers

Invite the children either to paint a raven or to make a flower picture.

For the ravens, you will need:
- a blank template of a raven
- black paint and brushes (and aprons)
- some white eyes or googly eyes to stick on
- a hole punch
- string to hang the birds

Ask the children to paint the ravens black—even their beaks—and stick on eyes. Punch a hole in the top and hang each bird from the ceiling with string.

For the flower pictures, you will need:
- bunch of flowers (preferably assorted)
- sticky-back plastic
- scissors to cut the plastic
- pieces of card

Ask the children to choose a flower. Take the petals off the flower and arrange them in a pattern on the card. When they've finished, place sticky-back plastic on top to keep the petals in place.

Ask...

Do you ever worry about things? What sorts of things do you worry about? (You could list the worries on a whiteboard or sheet of paper.)

Discuss...

Ask the children to imagine what it would be like not to worry about things. Would that be good? Would it be possible?

Examples: it's good to take care of things that we are able to take care of, like our personal belongings or our bodies, but it's not good to worry about really big problems.

What the Bible says: Luke 12:22–29

Story: Jesus tells people not to worry

Jesus told his friends not to worry about problems—even about the food they were going to eat or the clothes they were going to wear. Jesus told them that the most important thing is to love God. God knows they need help and will take care of them.

Jesus said, 'Look at ravens. They don't worry about storing up food to eat, because God looks after them.' He also said, 'Look at the wild flowers God made. Aren't they beautiful, even though they're not around for very long?' Jesus said that if God made flowers to be beautiful, he certainly cares about people, too.

What can we learn from the story?

Jesus said that it wasn't a good idea to worry about things, because worrying doesn't help to make them better. He said that God is big enough to take care of us and all our needs.

Reflection

When we have a problem that we can't solve, it's good not to worry but to let someone bigger than us, who cares about us, work it out instead.

Celebrations

Starter activity: Party!

Arrange a class party. Discuss when it's to be and what kind of food you're going to have. Make invitations, with everyone drawing and designing one. When the invitations have been made, they can all go into a hat. Then everyone from the class chooses an invitation, because everyone's invited. Maybe you could have some party games, too, and make your own party hats.

Ask...

Who's been to a party? What was it like? What sorts of things did you do? Did you eat nice food and play games? Were there presents? What made it fun?

Discuss...

Why do people have parties? Who gets invited?

> **Examples:** for birthdays at home or at different venues; for Christmas or to celebrate another event; friends and family or special guests.

What the Bible says: Matthew 22:1–10

Story: The king has a party

Jesus told a story about a king who invited everyone to a party. The king was celebrating his son's wedding. He was excited and sent invitations to all his friends. He told them it was going to be a great party with lots of yummy food.

Everything was ready. However, the first friends the king had invited said that they could not come, so the king sent out more invitations. This time the king decided that everyone who wanted to come could come. Soon the wedding party was full of celebrating guests and the king and his son were happy.

What can we learn from the story?

Jesus knew that everyone loves parties. He loved to celebrate, too, and was often invited to weddings and other celebrations. Jesus said that God is like the king in the story. God invites everyone to come to the party.

Reflection

Parties and celebrations are fun. It's good when we can include everyone in our parties and celebrations. Of course we all have special friends, but it's good to include others and to be included.

Confidence

Starter activity: Weight lifters

Make some fake weights. First, create a pole using rolled-up newspaper. Then add a balloon to each end. Have fun pretending to be really strong weight lifters who can lift anything, however heavy. Who can do the best impression of a weight lifter?

Ask...

If you had a problem, what would you do about it? What if someone could help you with your problem? Maybe it would be a bit like lifting your fake weights—not as bad as you first thought. You would feel a lot more confident.

Discuss...

What does it feel like to be confident at doing something? If you believe you can do something, does that make it easier to do?

What the Bible says: Ephesians 3:12

Story: Paul tells people to be confident

There was a man called Paul, who was a well-known Christian. He wrote lots of letters to other Christians to help them understand about God and Jesus. Some of these letters are in the Bible. In one, he explains to his friends that his special job of helping people was given to him by God. Paul had a lot of influence and people listened to him. However, he says that he often feels unworthy of such an important job. Despite feeling that way, he tells his friends that anyone can be confident about approaching God. It doesn't matter who they are or what is going on in their life: God still wants to listen, love them and help. Paul tells them to be confident that God listens to anyone who prays.

What can we learn from the story?

Paul wanted people to understand that even though God is amazing, big and powerful, he is still kind and loving and helpful. So everyone can be confident about praying and getting help. Even big problems are not big when God can help with them.

Reflection

When we are confident, we feel good, even doing things that look difficult at first. We can also ask for help. Lots of times, people want to help us, so we just need to ask. That makes us feel better.

Creativity

Starter activity: Clay animals

Give out coloured clay or Plasticine™ and ask the children to make a small clay animal. They can be as imaginative as they like. If they get stuck, they could make an animal they know, then add something unusual to it—making, for example, a pig with wings, a dog with six legs or a bird with human feet. When the animals have been made, invite the children to come up one by one to the front and tell the class what their animal's name is. Who can be the most creative?

Ask...

Think about the world. There are lots of things in it, aren't there? There are so many amazing animals and creatures in the world. What is your favourite animal or bird? What makes it special?

Discuss...

What would it be like if there were only one or two types of animals in the world? Do you think that the person who made the world was creative?

What the Bible says: Genesis 2:19–20

Story: God gets creative

At the beginning of the Bible, it says that God created the world and everything in it—all the animals, from big bears to tiny ants. Christians believe that God made them all and that he even involved the first human beings in naming the animals. In the story of creation, God brings animals and birds to the first human being to name. Can you imagine that?

What can we learn from the story?

Christians believe that God is really creative: you would need to be creative to make all the amazing things in the world. God likes to share good things with people and that includes being creative. God gives creativity to human beings, too.

Reflection

It's fun to be creative and there are lots of ways to do it—from making, drawing and painting to dancing and storytelling. Perhaps you have a favourite creative activity that you like to do. Have fun being creative!

 Reproduced with permission from *RE in the Classroom with 4–5s* by Helen Jaeger (Barnabas in Schools, 2015) www.barnabasinschools.org.uk

Curiosity

Starter activity: Windy day

Choose a windy day. Look out of the window together. Ask, 'Do you think it is windy today? Why do you think so? What things do you see moving in the wind?' Go outside together. Stand so that the wind blows in your face, then turn so that it blows on your side and then on your back. Talk about how the wind feels today. Does it blow steadily or does it stop and go? Is it a light breeze or a strong gust?

Find five things that are moving in the wind. Take a ribbon or a piece of paper. How does it move in the wind? What do you notice? What is making this object move? Listen to the wind and imitate the sounds that you hear.

Ask...

What does it mean to be 'curious'? When is it good to be curious?

> **Examples:** to learn new things; to discover; to explore; when you're on an adventure or in a new place.

Discuss...

What would happen if no one was curious? How does being curious lead to new things?

> **Examples:** doctors wouldn't invent new medicines; explorers wouldn't discover new places; scientists wouldn't learn new things; the police wouldn't catch criminals.

What the Bible says:
Luke 19:1–6

Story: Zacchaeus is curious about Jesus

Jesus came to a town called Jericho. In the town was a man called Zacchaeus. He wasn't very popular because he was a tax collector and he was very rich. Zacchaeus wanted to see Jesus, but he was a bit short, so he climbed up a tree to get a better look. As Jesus was going past the tree, he looked up and saw Zacchaeus. Jesus knew that Zacchaeus was curious about him and wanted to see him. Jesus was so kind that he told Zacchaeus he was going to come to his house for a party. Zacchaeus was overjoyed and quickly climbed down from the tree and welcomed Jesus into his house. He invited everyone else and there was a big party.

What can we learn from the story?

Zacchaeus wanted to see Jesus: he was curious about what Jesus was like. Zacchaeus didn't let the crowds or the fact that he was short put him off. He figured out a way to see Jesus. Jesus rewarded him: he invited himself to Zacchaeus' house.

Reflection

Sometimes it is good to be curious. It can help us to work out problems or solve puzzles. We may also experience something even better than we first thought.

Eating

Starter activity: Get fruity

Ask the children to see if they can rub their tummy and pat their head at the same time. Now ask them to swap hands. Is it easier one way or the other? Our tummies are really important. It's important to eat food that is healthy and good for us.

Ask everyone to think of their favourite healthy foods. What do they like? Maybe it's fruit, such as apples or pears. Or perhaps they like vegetables, such as carrots or broccoli. Draw pictures of these favourite healthy foods and colour them in. Stick the pictures on the wall—fruit in a giant fruit basket and vegetables in a saucepan.

Ask...

What is the class's favourite fruit and vegetable? Take a class poll.

Discuss...

How do you feel when you are really hungry? How do you feel when you have had something really nice to eat? What does healthy food do for you?

> **Examples:** you would be sad if you didn't have enough food to eat; you might not grow properly without it; when you have some yummy, healthy food, you feel happy and full of energy.

What the Bible says: Luke 9:12–17

Story: Jesus feeds 5000 people

One day, Jesus was teaching a large crowd in a faraway place. It was the end of the day, and Jesus' friends told Jesus that he should ask the people to find a place where they could get something to eat and stay for the night. But Jesus told his friends that *they* would feed the crowds. Jesus' friends thought he was crazy. How were they going to feed 5000 people? All they had was some pieces of bread and some small fish.

Jesus told his friends to ask the crowd to sit down. He took the bread and fish and prayed to God in heaven. His friends began to give the food out. Amazingly, it didn't run out—there was even some left over at the end.

What can we learn from the story?

Can you imagine 5000 people? That could be ten or even 20 times the number of people in your school. Everybody needs to eat. God knows that and cares about it. This is a story about God caring that people have enough food to eat.

Reflection

Eating healthy food regularly is really important. Try to make sure that you eat lots of different healthy foods at regular times this week.

Fairness

Starter activity: Rule challenge

Play a game that your class knows really well or has played before, but this time, change the rules without telling the class. What happens?

Ask...

What would it be like if people didn't play fair or changed the rules in the middle of a game?

Discuss...

Have you ever played a game where people changed the rules or weren't fair? What was it like? How can you make sure you are fair when you play together?

> **Examples:** make sure everyone knows the rules at the beginning; be kind if people forget the rules or don't know them; include people who want to play; listen to suggestions for new rules or ideas; always be truthful.

What the Bible says: Luke 15:11–32

Story: The man and his two sons

Jesus told a story about two brothers. They worked for their dad on his farm. They knew that when they were older, they would inherit the farm. It would be split 50/50 between them. But the younger brother couldn't wait. He wanted his share now. His dad said, 'OK' and gave him the money, but he was worried about his younger son. What would happen to him? Would he be all right?

Soon afterwards, the younger son set off from home. He spent all his money and then decided he should come home. He wasn't sure how his dad would treat him. Would he be angry? But his dad saw him from a long way off. He ran to his younger son. He was so happy to see him! He threw a party for him and told his servants to dress him in the best clothes. He was happy to have him home.

The older brother, who had never gone away, heard about the party and was very cross. His dad came to find him. 'Why are you cross?' he asked.

'I've worked really hard for you and you've never given me a party,' said the older brother. 'My younger brother goes away, spends all his money, comes home and you throw a party for him. It's not fair.'

'My son,' replied his father. 'Nothing's changed. Everything I own is yours! It's just that your younger brother has come home. It's right to celebrate that he's back safe and sound.'

What can we learn from the story?

God is interested in fairness and cares about how people feel. Of course, the dad in the story was very happy that his younger son had come home safe and sound, but he was also fair to his older son.

Reflection

Being fair is important. No one likes it when they think someone or something is unfair. It's always good to be fair, whether that's with your friends, at school or at home—but fairness doesn't always mean treating people exactly the same.

Family

Starter activity: Build together

You will need a chair for each child, and a stopwatch. Place the chairs in a circle and ask the children to sit down. Call out a formation, such as a cinema. The children must work together to move their chairs into that formation. When the formation is complete, the time is recorded. Then call out a new idea—for example, café, bus, circus, train, sitting room, football stadium or swimming pool.

Ask...

What's it like to build something together? Did you have fun?

Discuss...

What kinds of people make things together? What do they make?

> **Examples:** families; people in an office work together; builders build houses; people in a factory make things.

What the Bible says: Genesis 6:9—7:10

Story: Noah builds a big boat

There was once a man called Noah. He was a very good man who believed in God. Unfortunately the earth was full of bad things. God decided to send a flood to wipe it out and start again. But God didn't want to wipe Noah out, so God told Noah to build an ark—a very large boat—to save himself, his family and all the birds and animals. God gave the measurements for the boat to Noah, and Noah built it with the help of his family. When it was ready, Noah and his family got into the ark with all the animals and birds. God sent the flood as promised, but Noah and his family and all the animals and birds were safe in the ark until the flood had dried up.

What can we learn from the story?

Noah and his family worked together to build the ark, which saved them. When the ark was ready, they were all able to get inside it to be safe. God cares about families and God likes to look after everyone in a family.

Reflection

Being part of a family, whatever that family looks like, is a good thing. It's nice to have close family members, whether they are your mum or dad, brothers, sisters, cousins, aunties, uncles, grannies or grandads. Make a special point of saying thanks or giving a hug to a person in your family who you feel close to.

Fear

Starter activity: Shield

In old times, knights used shields to protect themselves when they went into battle. They decorated their shields with pictures of things that were important to them—a lion for courage, an eagle for sharp-sightedness or a dragon for power. They also used images such as hearts, fire, crosses, stars and suns. The colours had meaning: they used white for peace or blue for truthfulness. Sometimes they had words written at the bottom of their shields, too.

Give out shield templates to the children. Ask them to draw things on to their shields that are important to them. If they like football, they could draw a ball; if they like reading, a book; if they like computer games, a computer. If family is important, they could draw people; or they could draw a musical instrument if they like music. They can include as many items as they like, and they can use their favourite colours.

Ask...

Do you think knights would have been afraid of going into battle? They used their shields to protect themselves. It's normal to feel scared sometimes. When you are afraid, what helps you?

> **Examples:** feeling protected by someone or something; having a hug from someone who loves you; telling someone; laughing about it with a friend; sharing your fears; running away from a scary situation.

Discuss...

How many of you are afraid of things? What sorts of things are you afraid of?

What the Bible says: Psalm 28:7

Story: God is like a shield

The Bible says that God cares about us when we're afraid, and he wants to protect us. The Bible says that God wants to be our shield. The person who wrote these words knew what it was like to be scared, but knew that God was there to offer protection.

What can we learn from the story?

God wants to come between us and whatever we find scary, so that we're protected. Christians believe that God will never leave people alone and that he wants to protect and help—just as a shield would protect knights in battle.

Reflection

Having a shield reminds you that you don't need to be afraid. If you're afraid, why not tell someone bigger than you, who can help, just like Christians tell God when they're afraid and need protection.

Friends

Starter activity: Relay

Divide your class into roughly equal teams. Mark out a relay course and hand out batons or something similar to pass on. Remind the children that if anyone drops the baton, they have to go back to the start. Run the race to discover the winning team.

Ask...

Why is it nice to have a friend? What would it be like if you didn't have a friend? There are some things you can only do if you have friends—a bit like a relay race. What makes a good friend?

Discuss...

How can you be friendlier? How can you let your friends know that you like being friends with them?

> **Examples:** invite someone to sit next to you; save a place in the lunch queue; say thanks to your friends; invite them to your house; hold hands with your friend; play a game together.

What the Bible says: Matthew 4:18–22

Story: Jesus chooses his friends

One day Jesus was walking by a lake. He wanted some friends to help him with his work. He saw two brothers, called Simon and Andrew. They were fishing from the middle of the lake, and Jesus called to them. He invited them to come with him and be his special friends. They wanted to be friends with him, so they said 'yes'.

Jesus walked further on. He saw two more brothers, called James and John. They were mending their fishing nets. He invited them to be his friends, too, and they said 'yes'. Now Jesus was not alone. He had special friends to be with and share things with.

What can we learn from the story?

Over the next few years, Jesus and his friends did lots of things together. They became close and understood each other more and more. They laughed together, travelled to different places together, and helped each other when things were hard.

Reflection

It's good to have friends. Jesus knew this, which is why he invited people to be his special friends. Sometimes we ask other people to be our friends and sometimes they ask us. Everybody needs friends—even Jesus.

Fun

Starter activity: Crazy actions

Think of fun ways to do simple things. Walk around the classroom backwards or like a monkey. Speak gobbledegook to the person next to you. Give yourself a funny name and tell everyone what it is. Wear your jumper on your head. Talk really quickly. Write your name with your other hand. Tell a funny joke. Sit cross-legged on your chair.

Ask...

What's the most fun you have ever had? What were you doing? Who were you with? Why was it fun?

Discuss...

What is your favourite fun thing to do? What fun things could you do today?

What the Bible says:
John 2:1–11

Story: Jesus at a party

One day Jesus was at a wedding. It was a big party, with lots to eat and drink. But before the party was over, they had run out of wine. Jesus' mother was there, and she said to Jesus, 'They've run out of wine.' Jesus wanted to help the wedding party, so he did something very special. He turned seven jars of water into wine. The wine was so good that everyone was saying the party hosts had saved the best wine until last.

What can we learn from the story?

Jesus enjoyed going to parties and having fun with his friends, and cared about people having a good time. He didn't want the party to be spoilt, so he did something about it.

Reflection

It's good to have fun together. Parties are fun, especially when there is special food and drink to share, and they can make people feel happy.

Generosity

Starter activity: Bird bottle feeder

Each child will need a plastic bottle, a wooden stick (such as a chopstick or a blunt wooden skewer), string, scissors and bird feed.

Make two holes in the bottom of each bottle and thread some string through it to create a loop for hanging. Next, make a hole on each side, just below the top of the bottle. Push through the wooden skewer or chopstick to make the birds' perch. Finally, make several feeding holes above the perch, around the bottle. This is how the birds will access the bird feed. Children may need some assistance with making the holes. To save time in class, these could be prepared in advance.

Fill the feeders and hang them where they can be seen from the classroom, or invite the children to take them home with a bag of bird feed. You could have a bird identification book nearby.

Ask...

Can you remember a time when someone was generous to you? What happened? How did you feel? Did it make you feel good?

Discuss...

Can you think of a time when you were generous to someone else? Who was it? What did you do? How can you be generous to someone today?

> **Examples:** share your pens or a favourite game; invite someone into the lunch queue with you or to play a game.

What the Bible says: Matthew 5:43–48

Story: Jesus talks about God's generosity

One day Jesus was telling a story. Jesus said that God is very generous, sending sunshine and rain to all people—it doesn't matter whether they are good or bad. Jesus said he wanted his friends to be generous, too. Even when someone was mean to them, he wanted them to try to be generous, as God is. Jesus said that it's easy to be nice to your friends, who are nice to you, but it's much harder to be nice to people who are not nice to you.

What can we learn from the story?

Jesus knew that some people are easy to be friends with and other people are more difficult, especially if they are not so nice. However, Jesus wanted his friends to try to be nice to everyone they met.

Reflection

It's normal for us to like our friends, but maybe not to like some other people. Even though we all have special friends, who we like to be with, it's good to try to get on with everyone. That way, everyone is generous to everyone else, and that's much nicer.

 Reproduced with permission from *RE in the Classroom with 4–5s* by Helen Jaeger (Barnabas in Schools, 2015) www.barnabasinschools.org.uk

Growing

Starter activity: Plant a seed

Choose some simple seeds that you can plant and watch grow. Among the easiest are mustard and cress. You could make a cress head!

Use clean yoghurt pots that have had the wrappers peeled off. Glue on eyes, a nose and a mouth to make a face. Wet some scrunched-up kitchen roll and push it into the pot, followed by a thin layer of damp cotton wool, leaving a gap of about 2 cm below the top of the pot. Sprinkle a mixture of the mustard and cress seeds on top of the cotton wool, pressing them down lightly.

Leave the pot in a warm light place, and look daily for signs of growth. You should see something after about seven days. (Check that the cotton wool remains damp and add a little water, if necessary.)

Ask...

How many growing things can you name? What's the biggest or smallest natural thing you've seen growing? What makes them grow?

Discuss...

Have you ever seen anything start off small and grow into something bigger? What kinds of things grow?

> **Examples:** seeds; ants; acorns; trees; elephants; people; kitten or puppy.

What the Bible says: Luke 2:51–52

Story: Jesus grows up

The Bible says that Jesus was once a baby; then he was a child, like you, and finally he grew up to be a man. The Bible says that Jesus lived with his family, his mum and dad. He even had to do what they told him to do, just as you have to do what your parents or teachers tell you. As he grew up, he tried to do his best. The Bible says that Jesus learnt a lot as he was growing up, just as you are doing.

What can we learn from the story?

Jesus understands what it's like to grow up. He was once a child, too. He knows what it is like to have a family and to have to do what other people tell you to do. He probably played with his friends, as you do; he laughed, cried, ran around, went to bed and did all the things that children do.

Reflection

Lots of things in the world are growing—from seeds to people. Living things start off young and then become adult or older, like a lamb becoming a sheep or an acorn becoming an oak. This is the way that the natural world around us grows.

Guidance

Starter activity: Blind man's buff

Pick a child to be 'it'. Then choose four other people to help 'it' to catch the others. Put a blindfold on the first child and twirl them round three times. All the other children try to get as close to 'it' as possible. The helpers can shout instructions like 'Behind you' or 'Quick, grab them.' When someone is caught, 'it' tries to guess who they are, with guidance from the helpers. If the identity of the person is guessed, they become the new 'it', and the game continues.

Ask...

Did you ever need help to do something? Who helped you? How did they help you? Have you ever helped anyone else?

> **Examples:** showing someone the way; learning how to tie shoelaces; knowing where to put something away (like a packed lunch box) or where to find it (like a box of crayons).

Discuss...

What's the best thing to do when you don't know how to do something?

> **Examples:** ask someone who knows; look for clues; watch other people.

What the Bible says: Exodus 13:20–22

Story: God helps the Israelites to cross a desert

A long time ago, God's people, who were called the Israelites, had to make a journey across a big desert. It was very hard to know where to go, because all around them was sand. There were no signposts and they didn't know the way. God gave them a cloud to follow by day, and at night he gave them a fire to move in front of them. They needed guidance and God provided just the right kind.

What can we learn from the story?

God knew that the Israelites didn't know the way to go, and didn't want them to get lost. It was easy for them to see the cloud and the fire, because they were in the desert. The cloud and fire helped them to get to their destination safely.

Reflection

Sometimes we don't know how to do something, maybe because it's something new or something we have never done before. It's OK to ask for help or guidance. There are always people who can help us, just as God helped the Israelites.

Happiness

Starter activity: Happy song

Sing the following song with appropriate movements. (You can find the music online.)

If you're happy and you know it,
clap your hands (clap, clap).
If you're happy and you know it,
clap your hands (clap, clap).
If you're happy and you know it
and you really want to show it,
If you're happy and you know it,
clap your hands (clap, clap).

You could make up additional verses or ask the children to suggest ideas for different actions—for example, scratch your head; snap your fingers; twirl your arms; hug your friend; jump up high; slap your knees; touch your toes; fold your arms; do a dance.

Ask...

Can you remember a time when you were really happy? What were you doing? Who were you with? Why did you feel happy?

Discuss...

How many words can you think of that mean 'happy'? What do you do when you're happy?

> **Examples:** dance; sing; laugh; smile; jump about.

What the Bible says: James 5:13

Story: James talks to his friends about being happy

One day a man called James was writing a letter to his friends. He was explaining to them what they should do at different times. For example, he said that if anyone was ill, they should ask people to pray for them. If anyone was in trouble, they should ask God to help them. He also said that if anyone was happy, they should sing happy songs, especially songs saying how great God is.

What can we learn from the story?

One of the best feelings in the world is happiness. It's natural to show how happy we feel. James knew this and he wanted to tell people it was OK to show their happiness. One of the best ways of doing that, he said, was to sing a happy song of praise to God.

Reflection

Find a fun way to express your happiness. It doesn't matter if you're good at singing or not. It's just nice to express how happy you are. Sometimes it makes you even happier.

Health

Starter activity: Healthy picnic

Organise a healthy picnic with fun exercise thrown in. Find a suitable venue, outside the school or at a nearby park that you can walk to. Ask children to think of healthy snacks they could bring. You could try, for example:

- fruit (apples, pears, strawberries, bananas)
- low-fat dips (yogurt mixed with cucumber or honey)
- vegetables (carrot sticks, cucumber discs, peppers, celery, baby sweetcorn, spring onions or cherry tomatoes)
- cooked rice
- tortilla or pitta bread
- hummus
- tuna pasta
- potato salad
- low-fat cheese
- couscous and roasted vegetables
- flapjacks

Take plenty of water and add orange or lemon slices to it.

Choose games to play. Remember to take with you antiseptic handwipes, sun hats and cream, if necessary, and rubbish bags to collect any litter.

Ask...

What does it feel like when you're well? And when you feel poorly? Which is better?

Discuss...

What can you do to be healthy?

> **Examples:** brush your teeth; go to bed on time; get enough exercise; not watch too much television; eat healthy food and snacks.

What the Bible says: Isaiah 38:1–8

Story: King Hezekiah is very ill

One day King Hezekiah was very ill. He was so ill, he knew he was going to die. He was very sad. King Hezekiah prayed to God. He said, 'God, I want to live. Please help me.' God heard Hezekiah's prayer and decided to make him better. God sent Hezekiah a sign to know that his prayer had been heard, and made the sunlight go back ten steps on the stairs to Hezekiah's room. Hezekiah knew it was impossible for the sunlight to change by itself—it must have been God who did it. He was much happier and he also got better again.

What can we learn from the story?

God wants people to be healthy and cares when we are not. We all get poorly sometimes, but it's nice to be healthy. God cared about how ill Hezekiah was feeling. In this story, God makes Hezekiah well again.

Reflection

It is good to be healthy and it's good to look after our health—to eat healthy food, to exercise and to get enough sleep. That way, we can be as healthy as possible and look after ourselves.

Independence

Starter activity: Tree of life

Make some handprints using paint. Ask the children to think of one skill that they want to master, such as tying their shoelaces or learning the alphabet or counting to 100. Write or help them to write their goal on to their handprint. Create a tree with 'leaves' made from the handprints. Explain that, like a tree, we are all growing and learning new things.

Ask...

What sorts of things can you do by yourself? What sorts of things do you need help with? Do you have any older brothers or sisters? What sorts of things do they do that you would like to be able to do?

Discuss...

If there was one new thing you could learn how to do, what would it be? Can you make it your goal to try to be able to do it in a week or a month?

What the Bible says: Genesis 12:1–4

Story: Abram becomes independent

One day God spoke to a man called Abram. God said, 'Abram, leave your country and your family. Set out for a new land that I am going to show you. I want to make you into a great nation. I will bless you and do good things to you and for you.' God said that whoever respected Abram, God would respect, too.

What can we learn from the story?

Abram probably felt nervous, leaving his country and his family. He would have to be quite independent now, but Abram trusted God and knew that God wouldn't ask him to be independent unless it was because something good was going to happen as a result of it.

Reflection

Sometimes, it can be scary being independent and having to do things for ourselves. It's normal to feel nervous in new situations, but often it can lead to new, exciting, good things.

Kindness

Starter activity: Flower power

Give each child a circle cut out of coloured paper and some 'petals' (coloured paper in the shape of petals). Ask them to write the name of someone special or kind on the circle—for example, Mum, Dad, Nanny, or a favourite friend. Ask them to think of reasons why this person is special or kind—for example, 'lets me read books', 'helps me build dens', 'gives me hugs', 'loves me', 'plays games with me' and so on. Ask the children to write an idea on each of the petals.

Stick the circle and the petals together to make a flower. Give the flower to the special person as a gift.

Ask...

Have you ever been kind to someone? Has someone been kind to you? What happened? How did you feel?

Discuss...

How can you be kind to someone today? How can we be kind to each other in class, or at home? When else can we be kind?

> **Examples:** to mum or dad; to an annoying brother or sister; to a pet; to people in our class; to our teachers.

What the Bible says: Luke 10:30–37

Story: A kind stranger cares for an injured man

One day Jesus told a story about a man who got beaten up by robbers. The man was travelling along a road when he was suddenly ambushed by baddies. They beat him up, stole his clothes and his money and left him by the side of the road, half dead. A priest came walking down the road. He saw the beaten-up man but crossed over to the other side of the road. Another religious person came walking down the road. He saw the man who had been robbed but he didn't stop either. Finally, an ordinary person came walking down the road. He saw the man bleeding in the middle of the road and felt sorry for him, so he took him to get proper medical care and made sure the man got fully better.

What can we learn from the story?

In this story, who did you think would help the man—the religious people? They didn't. Jesus wanted to make it clear that anyone can be kind to anyone else. Even unlikely people can turn out to be kind and caring.

Reflection

It's good to be kind and caring, even to people we don't know. If we were in a situation where we needed help, like the beaten-up man in the story, think how grateful we would be. How can we be kind to others?

Learning

Starter activity: Densities

Explain to the children that different liquids can have very different densities. Density means the thickness or heaviness of something. This difference allows some liquids to float on top of others and some objects to float on some liquids. Which do they think is the heaviest out of the following list?

- treacle
- golden syrup
- water with a bit of food colouring
- vegetable oil

Pour the liquids above into a tall glass. They will settle into clearly visible layers, allowing you to talk about their different densities. To show that solids can be less dense than liquids, drop in a paperclip (which will float on the treacle layer) and a Lego™ brick (which will float on the water).

Ask...

What's the best thing you've ever learned? Did you enjoy learning it? What would you like to learn about next?

Discuss...

How can you become a really good learner? What makes someone good at learning?

> **Examples:** being curious; listening; watching; trying; practising; experimenting; concentrating.

What the Bible says: 2 Timothy 3:14–17

Story: Paul tells his friend, Timothy, how the Bible helps people to learn

One day Paul was writing a letter to his friend, Timothy. Timothy had spent a lot of time thinking about how to be a good Christian. He prayed and he read his Bible. Paul said it was good that Timothy read his Bible. Paul told Timothy that the Bible is a special book, with lots of useful stories and information that God has given to people. Paul said the Bible can help people who want to learn, and that learning the right way to live is a good thing.

What can we learn from the story?

Paul wanted Timothy to be strong in what he believed and to be able to do whatever good things he could in his life. Paul said that everyone can learn from the Bible, because the Bible comes from God.

Reflection

We all learn things. By learning, we get to know what is the right way to do something (and the wrong way too, sometimes). It's good to learn and to keep on learning.

Loyalty

Starter activity: Loyalty cards

Create membership cards for your classroom. You could use the name of your class or come up with a special name. Perhaps you could come up with a classroom logo—for example, pens and pencils, a star, or a mascot such as an animal or toy. Ask the children to put their name on their own card and sign it.

For fun, for the rest of the day, you could ask to see membership cards before anyone comes into the classroom. Anyone without a membership card (including teachers from other classes) will have to wait outside until they are allowed in.

Ask...

What does it mean to be loyal? Are you loyal to anything—for example, a football team? What do you do to show your loyalty?

Discuss...

How can you be loyal to people or things?

> **Examples:** not say bad things about them to anyone else; stick up for them if other people want to leave them out of a game; look after things; be nice to your friends; be reliable.

What the Bible says: 2 Samuel 9

Story: King David looks after his friend's family

King Saul had a son called Jonathan. David was his best friend. Saul and Jonathan died in battle, and David became king. When he became king, he asked Jonathan's disabled son, who was called Mephibosheth, to visit him. Mephibosheth was a little afraid. What could King David want with him? He didn't need to worry, though. David told him that he'd been best friends with Mephibosheth's dad and that he wanted to look after Mephibosheth now.

King David took Mephibosheth into his family and looked after him as if he was his own son. David was loyal to his old friend, Jonathan, and Mephibosheth was much happier.

What can we learn from the story?

David and Jonathan had been best friends and were very loyal to each other. One time, when David's life was under threat, Jonathan had helped him. David continued to be loyal to his friend, even when he was no longer around.

Reflection

Loyal friends stick with us through good and bad times. There are lots of things we like doing with friends. It's especially nice when someone is loyal to us: then we know that they are there for us and we are loyal to them, too.

Making mistakes

Starter activity: Snakes and ladders

Give a grid of squares to each child. Explain that they are going to design their own snakes and ladders game. They can include as many snakes and ladders as they like and make the snakes long or short. The only place they can't put a snake is on the final square.

Invite the children to play in pairs. At the end of the session, ask them what they did when they landed on a snake. Most of them will have carried on playing, despite the setback. Explain to them that that's exactly what we can do when we make a mistake—carry on and try to keep making progress.

Ask...

Have you ever made a mistake? What happened? What were you doing?

Discuss...

What's the best thing to do when you've made a mistake? If you make a mistake at home or school, what do you think you could do about it?

> **Examples:** tell someone; be honest; say sorry; make it up to someone; keep trying and don't give up; look at it as a chance to learn; pay more attention; ask for help.

What the Bible says: John 21:4–17

Story: Peter makes a mistake

One day, Peter was fishing with some of Jesus' other friends. A man from the lakeside called out, 'Friends, have you caught anything?' Peter and his friends said, 'No.' The man suggested they put their fishing net in a different spot—and they caught a massive number of fish. Peter realised that it was Jesus who was speaking to them. Jesus had died but had risen again.

When Jesus was going through a hard time, before he died, Peter had denied that Jesus was his friend. Now Peter jumped out of the boat and swam towards Jesus. Jesus and his friends shared breakfast together. After breakfast, Jesus asked Peter if he loved him. Peter said, 'Yes, of course, I really love you.' Jesus and Peter were friends again.

What can we learn from the story?

Peter made a big mistake when he said he didn't know Jesus. After all, Jesus loved him very much and was his best friend. Jesus wanted Peter to know it was OK to make mistakes, as long as he was sorry about it. They could be friends again.

Reflection

We all make mistakes. Sometimes we make big mistakes and sometimes we make small mistakes. It's OK to make mistakes, as long as we are sorry, are honest about them and try to make up for them. Making mistakes is part of life.

Making things

Starter activity: Tent city

Turn your whole classroom into a tent city or massive den. Divide the class into groups of three or four and make dens, using chairs, sheets, blankets, poles, tables and cushions. You could have a main road linking each of the dens and encourage friendly visits from other den-dwellers. Do the children have any suggestions to improve their designs? You could convert the mini dens into a main den in the middle of the classroom, which all the children work on, and have a storytelling session in it.

Ask…

What's the most fun thing you've ever made? What did it look like? What was it made out of? How did you get the idea for it?

Discuss…

Should we make something else together as a class? What could we make? What materials will we need? Who is going to do what jobs?

> **Examples:** create a mosaic wall, with lots of the children's artwork; build a temple, using decorated cereal or shoe boxes; plan a huge Lego™ build, with lots of different houses and buildings; plan a townscape, with roads, factories, houses, parks and fields that you make and colour in.

What the Bible says: 1 Kings 6 and 7

Story: King Solomon builds a temple

King Solomon was a very powerful and rich king who loved God. One day God asked him to do something special. God wanted a big temple, where everyone could come and pray and worship God. God wanted it to be very beautiful. God gave Solomon clear instructions about what the temple should look like. Some of it would be made of big blocks of stone with wood laid over the top. There would even be decorations of things like angels, palm trees, lions, bulls and flowers. Solomon used gold, silver and bronze in the design. How long do you think it took to build? It took seven years.

What can we learn from the story?

Solomon listened to what God said and made a plan. When Solomon started to build the temple, the builders had to stick to the plan. The king used God's plan to decide what would go in the temple and how it would look. There were lots of people working on the project together.

Reflection

Making things can involve lots of stages, from having an idea to planning it out, to making it and completing it—and it can involve lots of people. It's good to work together to make things.

Moving

Starter activity: Dance and move

Put on some music and let everyone dance. At intervals, suddenly stop the music and shout an instruction, like 'jump three times', 'spin round', 'face the opposite wall', 'turn to your right', 'turn to your left' or 'find a partner'. Keep going until everyone is tired.

Ask...

What was it like when the music stopped and you suddenly had to do something new? What was it like to move in a different way? Did you enjoy it? Was it fun or tiring?

Discuss...

Sometimes it's fun to move in a different way and sometimes it can be a little bit tiring. Changing around like this can be confusing, too. When you're going through changes, it can be a mixed experience. What makes it easier?

> **Examples:** moving house or school; having someone show you what to do; having someone help you.

What the Bible says: Exodus 7—12

Story: The Israelites move

The Israelites were slaves in Egypt. They were treated very badly and were miserable. They prayed to God, and God chose Moses to lead the people out of Egypt. Moses went to the leader of Egypt, Pharaoh, and asked him to let the Israelites go. Pharaoh said 'No.' God told Moses he would help them. God filled the land with frogs, flies and insects to get Pharaoh to change his mind. Pharaoh said 'No.' God sent diseases on the cattle and sheep and they all got sick. Pharaoh said 'No.' Next there was a terrible hailstorm and darkness that lasted for three days. God sent one last plague on Egypt—the death angel. Every firstborn in Egypt died. Finally Pharaoh let the Israelites go. God led the Israelites out of Egypt to a new land that would be their own, where they would no longer be slaves.

What can we learn from the story?

The Israelites were having a very hard time in Egypt. They were being treated badly. God was concerned about them and wanted them to live in their own country, where they would be happy. God helped the Israelites to move.

Reflection

Sometimes we go through changes—moving house, going to a new school, leaving nursery. Change and moving can be difficult at first, but later they can be good for us.

Obedience

Starter activity: 'Simon says...'

Play a game of 'Simon says'. Everyone must obey a command that begins with 'Simon says'—for example, 'Simon says... touch your toes / rub your nose / jump in the air.' But everyone must ignore a command that starts without 'Simon says'. Players are out if they get it wrong. The winner is the last child left in.

Ask...

What would it be like if no one was obedient? Would that be OK or would it be a problem?

Discuss...

When is it good to be obedient? How is it helpful to be obedient? Who do we need to be obedient to?

> **Examples:** to keep us safe; at school and at home; in a club or playing sport; to our teachers, parents and people who are looking after us or are in charge.

What the Bible says: Deuteronomy 30:11–16

Story: Moses gives the Israelites a choice

After God had led the Israelites out of Egypt, where they had been slaves, they came to a new land. God wanted to give this new land to them. Moses was the leader of the Israelites. He said to them, 'God wants to bless you, but you need to obey God. It's not difficult to do what God wants. The most important thing is to be obedient. If you do this, good things will happen to you and God will look after you.' Moses told the people that they needed to love God, be obedient and keep his rules, which were rules to help them and give them life and make them happy.

What can we learn from the story?

God gave the people clear instructions to obey. They weren't difficult rules to understand—they were easy. God wanted people to do the right thing, so that good things would happen to them.

Reflection

When we are obedient, things tend to go better for us. It is good to listen to instructions and to do the right thing.

Patience

Starter activity: Go fishing

Put the children in groups. Ask each group to draw or design a fish on a piece of card and attach a paperclip to it. Take a stick, such as a chopstick or pencil, tie a piece of string around it, and add a small magnet to the piece of string. Place the fish on the table or on a blue piece of paper to represent the sea or a lake. Have a go at trying to catch the fish using the fishing rods. You might need to be patient!

Ask...

Have there been times when you have had to be patient? What happened? How do you feel, having to wait for something? Is it easy or hard?

> **Examples:** waiting for Christmas or a birthday; it can be easy or hard, exciting or frustrating.

Discuss...

Can you imagine a time when it's good to be patient? When do you need to be patient at school and at home?

> **Examples:** it's more fun to discover what your Christmas present is on the day than beforehand; learning a new skill; sharing or taking turns.

What the Bible says: John 21:1–6

Story: Peter learns patience

One day Peter and his friends went fishing. They fished all through the night, but they didn't catch a thing—not even a tiny shrimp! They were very disappointed. They'd worked hard all night. Just as they were about to give up, Jesus appeared. He said to them, 'Don't worry, have one last go!' They trusted Jesus. Even though they were tired of trying to catch fish, they had one last go. Guess what? They caught so many fish, their nets began to break and they had to call over other fishermen to help them pull all the fish into the boat. They were amazed!

What can we learn from the story?

Jesus wanted his friends to learn about patience. Sometimes we give up too easily or too quickly. Jesus wanted his friends to know that patience is good and helps us to manage whatever we're trying to do. Not everything happens immediately.

Reflection

Sometimes we can try to do something and it just doesn't work. We want to give up. But maybe it's better to give it one last go. Who knows, we might succeed on our last go!

Paying attention

Starter activity: Chinese whispers

Each child takes it in turns to whisper a sentence to the child next to them. Choose a simple sentence— for example, 'The sky is blue today' or 'All mice like cheese'. Whisper the sentence into the first child's ear and ask them to pass it on. The whisper follows the circle, ending back with the teacher, who repeats whatever is heard to the whole class. (It's usually not the original sentence!)

Ask...

What would it be like if no one paid attention?

Discuss...

When is it important to pay attention?

> **Examples:** for road safety; when a parent or carer says something important; when playing a game with friends.

What the Bible says: 1 Samuel 3:1–10

Story: Samuel pays attention to God

When Samuel was a young boy, his mother sent him to help at the temple. Eli lived there. He was the priest. One night, Samuel heard someone calling him. He thought it was Eli, so he got out of bed and went to Eli. 'Here I am,' he said, but Eli said, 'I didn't call you. Go back to bed.' Again, Samuel heard a voice calling him. He got out of bed and ran to Eli. Again, Eli sent him back to bed.

Eli told Samuel that if he heard the voice calling his name again, he should say, 'Speak, Lord, I am listening.' Again Samuel heard a voice calling him, so he did as Eli said. Samuel grew up and became a famous person in Israel, because he paid attention to God.

What can we learn from the story?

Samuel paid attention when he heard someone calling his name. He was very obedient. He ran to Eli first of all, because he thought he was calling him, but it turned out that God wanted to speak to Samuel.

Reflection

Listening is good for everyone, especially when someone has something important to say.

Peace

Starter activity: Visualisation

Choose some relaxing music to play. Ask the children to make themselves comfortable and close their eyes. They can lie on the floor, sit with their heads on their arms or make themselves feel restful in some other way. Explain that you are going to play some peaceful music and ask them to imagine that they are in a peaceful place. You could guide them by reading out a description of somewhere like a field in the sunshine, floating on a cloud, staring at the sky or even lying in their own bed.

Guide them to relax their own bodies, starting with their toes and working their way through their body, all the way up to their heads. Invite them to feel floppy, peaceful and relaxed.

Ask...

What does it feel like when you feel peaceful? What kinds of things do you do to feel peaceful? Are there times of the day or activities that make you feel especially peaceful?

> **Examples:** I feel calm and secure; I like to listen to music or watch my favourite television programme; I feel peaceful at bedtime, when I am warm in my bed.

Discuss...

How can we make our school or home more peaceful?

> **Examples:** listen to each other; not argue; be understanding and help someone if they are confused or scared; do, watch or listen to things that make us feel peaceful.

What the Bible says: John 20:19–21

Story: Jesus gives his friends peace

When Jesus died on the cross, his friends didn't know what to do. They shut themselves away in a room. After Jesus rose from the dead, he appeared to his friends in the room where they were hiding, walking through a closed door. They couldn't believe it. Jesus knew they were confused and scared, but he loved them very much. He said, 'Don't be afraid. I want you to feel peaceful—as peaceful as I am.' Jesus gave his friends a special gift—the gift of peace.

What can we learn from the story?

Jesus wanted to give his friends the gift of peace. He didn't want them to be afraid or confused any more.

Reflection

Sometimes we can go through confusing experiences or times that are a bit scary. It's good if we can try to feel peaceful and make things peaceful for other people.

Playing

Starter activity: Board games

Have a game-playing day. Invite the children to bring in their favourite board games. Have fun playing each other's games and learning new games.

Ask...

What's your favourite game to play? Do you like to include other people in your games? What is it like when someone invites you to play a game with them? How does it feel?

Discuss...

How can we make our home or classroom a place where everyone feels included and can play together? What sorts of things could we do to make that happen?

> **Examples:** invite people to play with us; share things with others; not be mean and tell people to go away if they want to play with us.

What the Bible says: Matthew 19:13–15

Story: Jesus likes children

One day some people brought their children to Jesus. They wanted to bring their children close to Jesus, but some of Jesus' followers had a problem with this. They didn't want the people to bring their children to Jesus. They thought the children were too noisy. They told off the parents and asked them to go away, but Jesus stopped them. He said, 'No, I want the children to come to me. Please don't stop them. My kingdom belongs to everyone, including children.'

His followers said 'sorry' and let the children come to Jesus. Jesus hugged the children and blessed them.

What can we learn from the story?

Jesus wanted everyone to come to him: no one was left out. Jesus liked the children as they were, and liked it when they played together, too. He didn't want people to be serious all the time, and he wanted everyone to know that they were welcome and included.

Reflection

It's good when we can welcome and include everyone in our games, giving everyone the chance to play.

Presents

Starter activity: Pass the parcel

Wrap a small gift in layers of recycled coloured paper or newspaper. Ask the children to sit in a circle, and explain that they must pass the parcel around the circle. Play music and turn it off at random intervals. When the music stops, the child who is holding the parcel unwraps a layer. Whoever unwraps the final layer keeps the gift.

> **Variations:** you could include a small gift in every layer, so that each child who unwraps receives something, or you could include a note of something for the child to do—a mime, song or dare.

Ask...

At which special times in the year do we give and receive presents? What's the best present you've ever had? When did you receive it? Who gave it to you? How did you feel?

> **Examples:** Christmas, Easter or birthday; new toy; given by family or friends; happy or excited.

Discuss...

How can we be more giving? How can we show someone we care about them by giving them a gift? What kind of gifts could we give?

> **Examples:** we can give things, but also do little things, like chores; give hugs; say 'thank you'.

What the Bible says:
Luke 1:26–38

Story: An angel visits Mary

There was a woman called Mary, who loved God. One day an angel visited Mary. The angel told her that she was going to have a special baby. When Mary saw the angel, she was afraid, but the angel said, 'Do not be afraid. God loves you. He wants to give you a son. The baby will be God's son. You must call the baby Jesus.' Mary was amazed. She asked the angel, 'How can this be true?' The angel said to her, 'Nothing is impossible with God.' Mary was full of joy at the angel's news.

What can we learn from the story?

God likes to give good gifts to people. He gave Jesus to Mary because he loved Mary very much. Jesus was a very special person. He wasn't just a gift to Mary; he was a gift to the whole world, too.

Reflection

It's good to give presents and to receive them, too. People give presents to people they love and care about. It's exciting to get a present, and it can be exciting to give a present, too.

Respect

Starter activity: Lion masks

You will need:

paper plates; yellow wool; yellow, black and orange tissue paper; black card; marker pens; hole punch; (elastic) string; scissors.

First, cut two round shapes out of the paper plate, for eyes. Next, cover the paper plate with yellow and orange tissue paper, like the fur of a lion. For the lion's mane, glue on yellow wool. Cut a black triangle for the lion's nose. Use the marker to make a mouth. Punch holes in the sides of the plate and thread the string through, to help the masks stay in place.

Why not act out the story of Daniel (see below)? Instead of eating him, the lions can be friendly—perhaps lying near him, purring or stroking him with their paws.

Ask...

What does it mean to respect someone? How can you show respect to someone? What kinds of people do we need to respect?

Examples: listen to what they say; take them seriously; do what they say; parents, teachers, police, other adults and each other.

Discuss...

How does it help us when we respect people? Is it a good or bad thing?

Examples: respecting rules helps to keep us safe; respecting other people means we get on with them.

What the Bible says: Daniel 6:1–23

Story: Daniel is protected in the lions' den

Daniel lived in a country called Babylon. Daniel loved God and prayed to God every day. God loved Daniel, too. The king of Babylon made Daniel a leader, but other people were jealous of Daniel and wanted to get rid of him. They made a law saying that it was wrong to pray to anyone but the king. If anyone did it, they should be thrown to the lions.

Daniel respected God, and he kept on praying. The jealous people took Daniel to the king and said that Daniel had broken the law. The king was sad. He knew he'd been tricked, but he had to do what the new law said. As Daniel was taken to the lions' den, the king said, 'May God rescue you.'

The next day, the king hurried to the lions' den. He called out, 'Daniel, did God save you?' Daniel replied, 'Yes, God saved me. The lions did not hurt me!'

What can we learn from the story?

Daniel respected God. God looked after Daniel. Even when Daniel was thrown to the lions, God looked after him—he wasn't even scratched. Daniel respected the king, too. After all, he was in charge. Everything was all right in the end.

Reflection

It's good to have respect, especially for good people who look after us. Sometimes, people we respect protect and look after us, like our parents or our teachers.

Rest

Starter activity: Sleeping dogs

Play a game of sleeping dogs. Discuss what dogs like to do—run around, chase a ball, bark, and so on. Explain that everyone can pretend to be a dog, but when the whistle blows they must lie down and be very still, just like a dog having a sleep. If anyone moves, they will be out. Blow the whistle to start the game again. Play until there is a winner.

Ask...

Do you like to have a rest? When you've done some hard work, what's your favourite thing to do?

> **Examples:** sit down; watch television; have a nap; play a game; read a book; eat a snack; sleep.

Discuss...

What would happen if people didn't rest? Would that be good or bad? Could it be dangerous for certain people?

> **Examples:** people might get grumpy or miserable; could be dangerous for people in charge of things, like a train driver or a doctor making complicated decisions.

What the Bible says: Genesis 2:1–4

Story: God has a rest

In the Bible, it says that it took God six days to create the world, and on the seventh day he had a rest. God said that having a rest was a good thing to do. It was so good that God wanted everybody who worked to have a rest, too. That's why God said the seventh day was a day just to rest, with no hard work. He blessed the seventh day, because it was good.

What can we learn from the story?

God knew that everyone gets tired after doing lots of hard work. Even God needed to rest after making the world. God wants to make sure we get enough rest.

Reflection

It's good to take a break after we've done a lot of work. Sometimes we have a break from studying or working, like at school when we have break time and lunch time. We go to bed and sleep the whole night. At weekends, we often have a full day of rest, so that we're refreshed and ready for the new week ahead.

Rules

Starter activity: Gingerbread biscuits

Show the children some gingerbread biscuit dough. This can be purchased at most major supermarkets, or recipes can easily be found on the internet. Explain that you need to follow a recipe to get it right. Share the dough among the children for them to roll out and cut shapes, and let them choose decorations to add at home. These could include:

- raisins for eyes (add before baking)
- cinnamon drops or sweets for mouth
- chocolate drop buttons
- icing sugar and water for 'glue' (or use plain and coloured tubes of icing paste)

Ask...

What kind of rules do you have at home or at school? Who sets the rules? Do you think they are good rules? Why? Explain that having a recipe is a little like having rules. If you follow the recipe, you are successful, and if you don't follow the recipe, it can all go wrong.

> **Examples:** get enough sleep; don't eat too many sweets; be quiet when someone is talking; do what your mum or dad tells you to do; don't run across the road; don't talk to strangers.

Discuss...

What kind of rules shall we have in our classroom? Can we think of three rules that would help everyone?

> **Examples:** be nice to everyone; say please and thank you; don't run in the classroom.

What the Bible says: Exodus 20:1–17

Story: God gives ten good rules

One day God called Moses to the top of a big mountain. Moses was the leader of the Israelites. God had a special message for Moses. God wanted to give Moses ten commandments, or rules, for the people to obey. God knew that these ten rules would make the people happy because they would help people to be nice to each other and to love each other, as God loved them.

What can we learn from the story?

Sometimes we don't know what is the best thing to do, but rules can help us to understand. God's rules were very simple but they were good rules to live by.

Reflection

We all need rules to help us live with each other. Sometimes people have different ideas about what is a good thing to do, but rules can help us to get along with each other and know the right thing to do.

Safety

Starter activity: Hidden butterflies

Camouflage helps insects to avoid being eaten by birds, letting them blend in with their surroundings so that dangerous predators can't find them. For example, a green grasshopper is hard to spot on a green leaf, and a white mountain rabbit can blend into a snowy hillside.

Give each child a butterfly template. Ask them to decide where they might hide it and then colour it in, choosing colours that will help it to blend into its surroundings. Each child writes their name secretly on the back of their butterfly and hides it. Then let everyone play hide and seek. Who made the best camouflage butterfly?

Ask...

What sorts of things do you do to stay safe? Are there dangerous situations you need to avoid?

> **Examples:** wear bright clothing on winter nights; always hold someone's hand when crossing the road.

Discuss...

How can we make our classroom safe for everyone? Sometimes, not doing something helps us to stay safe.

> **Examples:** don't run with scissors or paint; put chairs under tables; mop up any spills quickly; tidy away bags so that people don't fall over them.

What the Bible says: Matthew 2:1–12

Story: Wise men visit Jesus

One day three wise men were looking at the stars. They saw a very bright star. They knew it was special—it meant a new king had been born. Who could it be? They followed the star and eventually reached Israel. They went to see King Herod. 'Where is the new king?' they asked. 'I don't know,' said Herod.

Herod was a bad king, and he decided to trick the wise men. 'Please follow your star and then come back and tell me where this new king is, so that I can worship him, too,' he said. The wise men followed the star and came to Bethlehem. They found Mary and the baby Jesus. They gave Jesus gifts of gold, frankincense and myrrh. The three wise men were going to return to Herod, but God gave them a dream. God said, 'Don't go back to Herod. He wants to kill the baby!'

The wise men went home by a different road and the baby Jesus was saved.

What can we learn from the story?

God knew that if Herod found out about Jesus, he would try to kill him, so God sent a dream to the wise men to tell them what to do.

Reflection

Being safe and protected is a good thing. It's important not to get ourselves into trouble when we don't need to be.

Security

Starter activity: Build a house

You could build houses out of cardboard boxes, tubing, tape and paint, with the children working in pairs or groups. Ask the children to paint their house, make a roof, glue the pieces together and then add details, such as windows and doors.

Alternatively, you could have some sand-play time. Ask the children to build sandcastles and sandhouses together in groups, and then watch them get washed away as someone pours water over them (like in the story below).

You could do both activities and ask, 'Which type of house is more secure?' Read the story of the three little pigs who built houses of straw, wood and bricks, with the big bad wolf trying to blow each house down.

Ask...

What is the most solid substance to make things out of? Is it paper, water, sand or rock? If you were building a house, where would you build it, and what would you build it from?

> **Examples:** build from brick or rock; build away from rivers that flood; make sure the doors and windows shut tight; use good-quality materials.

Discuss...

What kinds of things make us feel secure? How can we make our classroom a place where people feel secure and happy?

> **Examples:** follow the rules; be nice to each other; listen and do what is right.

What the Bible says: Matthew 7:24–27

Story: Sensible and silly builders

Jesus told a story about two people who were building houses. The first man was sensible: he built his house on rock. Then a big storm came. It rained, the river flooded and there was a very strong wind, but the sensible man's house was secure because he had built it on a solid foundation. There was another man. He was silly: he built his house on sand. A big storm came. It rained a lot, the river flooded and there was a very strong wind—and the silly man's house fell down because he had built it on a weak foundation.

What can we learn from the story?

Jesus said that people who listened to his words and put them into practice were like the sensible builder. They were building their lives on a good, solid foundation.

Reflection

Doing the right thing helps us to feel secure. Even if we have problems (like the big storm in the story), we will be more confident and peaceful about them.

Sharing

Starter activity: Conga!

Dance the conga together. Invite one child to be a leader and move past all the other children, who are standing still. As the leader passes each child, that child puts their hands on the shoulders or waist of the child in front of them and joins the dance. Put music on and have the leader move the conga line around the room.

Ask...

Do you like to share? What sorts of things do you like to share? Who do you like to share them with?

> **Examples:** food; games; pens; brothers and sisters; friends.

Discuss...

How can we share in our classroom? What sorts of things can we do?

> **Examples:** lend something to someone when they ask to borrow it; offer help to someone.

What the Bible says: Ruth 1:1–18

Story: Ruth shares with Naomi

Naomi moved to a land that was far away. Her sons married women there, but her husband and her sons died, and Naomi wanted to go home. She told her sons' wives to go home to their families, too, but one of the women, called Ruth, said she would follow Naomi. She loved her mother-in-law and didn't want to leave her. So the two women travelled back to Naomi's home in Israel. At first things were hard, but Ruth worked and found enough food for them both to live on. Later Ruth met and married a man called Boaz. They had a baby boy, called Obed, and everyone was happy again.

What can we learn from the story?

Ruth decided she would share her life with Naomi. Naomi had lost her husband and her sons. Ruth didn't want her to lose anything else. She wanted to be with Naomi and share with her. God did good things for Ruth and Naomi.

Reflection

Sometimes, when we share with other people, we end up receiving good things, too. When we are generous and caring, people are more likely to be generous and caring to us.

Specialness

Starter activity: Special sheep

Cut out templates of sheep. Ask the children to stick cotton wool on to the body of each sheep. On the back of the sheep, each child can write their name and something that makes them special—for example, 'I'm good at football', 'I'm fun', 'I like reading', and so on. It can be anything that makes them feel special.

Ask...

What makes you special? What makes your friend special? Even though we are in a class together, like a flock of sheep, each one of us is special.

Discuss...

How can we make each other feel special?

> **Examples:** ask about each other; find out if someone is OK, especially when they are missing from class or school; sing 'Happy birthday' on someone's birthday; give someone a compliment.

What the Bible says: Luke 15:3–7

Story: The lost sheep

One day Jesus told a story about a lost sheep. The shepherd was very worried. He had counted his sheep. Normally there were a hundred, but today there were only 99. Where was his lost sheep? He knew there was a sheep missing, so he left the other 99 sheep and went to look for the lost one. Eventually he found it. He was so happy! He put the sheep on his shoulders and carried it home.

When he got home, he called all his friends and neighbours. He said, 'Look, I've found my lost sheep. Let's have a party to celebrate!' All the shepherd's friends agreed. Best of all, the sheep was no longer lost but snug and warm at home with the other sheep.

What can we learn from the story?

Jesus said that each person is special, just like that one lost sheep. God cares about every single person and, just like the shepherd, God wants everyone to be safe and happy.

Reflection

Sometimes we can think that other people are more important or more popular, or better at doing things, like playing football or writing their name neatly, than we are. But we're all special. We have special talents and gifts and we're special, just because we're who we are.

Sticking up for others

Starter activity: Straw puppets

Make some straw puppets. Cut out pictures of people or characters from a magazine, glue a picture on to cardboard and tape a straw to the back.

Put the children into groups of three and ask them to make up a story about someone who is having a hard time. Perhaps someone else is saying nasty things to them or trying to hit them, or it could be someone who has fallen over in the playground. The other puppet or puppets stick up for the one who needs help. Act out the stories.

Ask...

Have you ever stuck up for someone? What happened? Who was it? How did it turn out? Has anyone stuck up for you?

> **Examples:** a friend who has had something nasty said to them; someone who hurt themselves and needed help.

Discuss...

What can we do to stick up for other people? What if someone hurts themselves at school? What do we do about it?

> **Examples:** find a teacher or adult and get help; be caring and kind to each other; look out for each other.

What the Bible says: John 11:1–44

Story: Mary and Martha's brother Lazarus needs help

There was once a man called Lazarus. He had two sisters who were called Martha and Mary. Lazarus got very ill, so his sisters sent a message to Jesus, who was their friend. They said, 'Our brother is very sick' and asked him to come.

Jesus waited for two days. When he finally got to his friends' house, Lazarus had died. Martha said to Jesus, 'Why didn't you come? Lazarus is dead.' They were very sad. Mary was crying.

Jesus went to the tomb where Lazarus had been laid. He said, 'Lazarus, come out!' and Lazarus walked out of the tomb. Lazarus was alive again!

What can we learn from the story?

Mary and Martha were worried about their brother because he was so ill. They sent a message to Jesus, because they knew Jesus could help. Even though Jesus didn't come at once, he was able to raise Lazarus from the dead.

Reflection

It's good to stick up for others, particularly when they can't help themselves or when we are asking someone to help them.

Stories

Starter activity: Make a story book

For each child, fold two sheets of A4 paper in half and staple them together at the fold to create an eight-page A5 booklet. Ask the children to choose a simple subject, such as 'my family', 'my favourite game' or 'what I did at the weekend'. Alternatively, create an imaginative story.

Encourage the children to write about their subject and to draw and colour in pictures. You could look at magazines and story books to get ideas, or use pictures from the magazines.

Hang the story books up in a story book corner. Invite the children to read each other's stories.

Ask...

Do you have a favourite book? What's it called? What's your favourite story, and why?

Discuss...

Who likes to listen to stories? Have you ever made up a story of your own? What happened in it?

What the Bible says: Mark 4:1–32

Story: Jesus teaches the crowds

One day Jesus was teaching by a lake. There were so many people that he had to get into a boat. Jesus stood in the boat and taught the people. He told many stories about different things. On this day, he told some stories about seeds, because he knew the people would understand. The first story was about a man who went to sow some seeds in a field. The second story was about a man who went to bed at night and was amazed when the seeds in his field sprouted. The third story was about a mustard seed, which is very tiny but grows to become a huge tree, for all the birds to rest in.

What can we learn from the story?

The people wanted to learn how to live good lives, and they needed a teacher. Jesus was a very good teacher. He told stories so that everyone who was listening could understand. They liked to be in Jesus' school, and Jesus liked to use stories to teach people.

Reflection

It's good to learn, and there are lots of different ways to do it. Hearing or reading a story is a fun way to learn.

Talents

Starter activity: Size 'em up!

Draw some simple shapes of common objects in a grid on a piece of paper, in random order—for example, a spoon, a mug, a television, a house, an elephant and an aeroplane. Photocopy the sheets and give one copy to each child, along with a pair of scissors. Ask them to cut out the shapes and put them into size order. Is the smallest thing more useful than the biggest? No. Everything has value. Everything is useful for doing something.

Ask...

Who has a special talent? What is it? Can you tell what other people's talents are?

> **Examples:** football; music; singing; being kind; drawing; swimming; being friendly; being funny; remembering things.

Discuss...

How can we use our talents? Have you used your talent and learnt something else?

> **Examples:** enjoy using talents regularly, like swimming every week or practising football; learn a new skill, like how to play a musical instrument; learn how to look after a pet.

What the Bible says: Matthew 25:14–30

Story: Servants and talents

One day Jesus told a story. He said that there was a king who went on a long journey. Before the king went away, he summoned three of his servants. To one servant he gave ten gold coins (called 'talents'), to the second servant he gave five, and to the third servant he gave one. The king said to all three servants, 'Use this money wisely.'

When the king returned from his journey, he called the three servants to him. To the first one, he said, 'What did you do with my money?' The servant said, 'I put it to use and made ten more talents for you. Here they are,' and he gave the king 20 talents. 'Well done,' said the king. 'I know I can trust you. I am going to put you in charge of ten cities.'

Then the king called the second servant. 'What did you do with my money?' he asked. 'I put your money to work and made five more talents for you. Here they are,' he said, and gave the king ten talents. 'Well done,' said the king. 'I know I can trust you. I am going to put you in charge of five cities.'

The king then called the third servant. 'What did you do with my money?' he asked. The third servant was afraid, because he hadn't done anything. 'I know you are a tough king,' said the servant, 'so I put your money away in a cloth.'

'What?' asked the king. 'You didn't even put it in a bank, to earn some interest?' 'No, I didn't,' said the third servant. 'That's very bad!' exclaimed the king. Then he said to other servants standing nearby, 'Take this servant's one coin and give it to the servant who has ten!'

What can we learn from the story?

Jesus wanted people to understand that everyone has special gifts. He wanted them to understand that it's good to use our talents. Sometimes, when we learn one new thing, it leads to another.

Reflection

It doesn't matter what talents we have, however big or small. The important thing is that we use the talents we have.

Teaching

Starter activity: What made this?

Write the word 'tool' on the whiteboard or on a big piece of paper. Think of the names of different tools—hammer, saw, screwdriver, spanner, wrench. (If you have a construction corner, you could show plastic tools and ask for their names.) What does a tool do? A tool can be something that you use to build something else with.

Next, divide the class into small groups. Ask them to choose one object in the room, such as a table or a chair, and then write or draw on their piece of paper the tools they think would have been used to make that object. Ask them to examine the object really carefully and come up with as many tools as they can think of. Which object needs the most tools to make it?

Ask...

People are a bit like tools: they have a job to do, too. What kind of jobs can you think of? How many jobs can you list?

> **Examples:** what your mum or dad does; what people around you do; what people at school do.

Discuss...

What is the job of a teacher? What things does a teacher do?

> **Examples:** helps people to learn; explains new things; answers questions; helps people to behave properly.

What the Bible says: Luke 11:1–4

Story: Jesus teaches his friends

One day Jesus was praying. When he finished praying, one of his friends said to him, 'Jesus, please teach us how to pray.' Jesus said, 'This is how you should pray. Say, "Our Father, hallowed be your name; your kingdom come, your will be done on earth as in heaven. Give us today our daily bread and forgive us our sins, as we forgive people who sin against us. And lead us not into temptation."' Jesus taught his friends all the things they needed to say in prayer.

What can we learn from the story?

Jesus was a good teacher. He was patient and kind and he always answered questions that people asked him, especially when they were trying to learn something.

Reflection

Teachers are important people. They help us to understand things and to know what to do. Good teachers give us the answers we need.

Truth

Starter activity: Truth or dare?

In advance, draw up a list of safe 'truth or dare' questions. Sit the children in a circle and choose a way of nominating a child to play the game. Here are some examples of questions.

Dare

- Hop on one leg for 20 seconds.
- Run around wearing socks on your hands.
- Lick your elbow while saying the alphabet.
- Do a silly dance with no music.
- Do a ballet dance.
- Try to rub your tummy while patting your head.
- Sing a song.
- Whistle or click your fingers.

Truth

- What is your favourite type of clothing?
- What is the name of your teddy bear?
- What is your middle name, if you have one?
- If you woke up invisible one day, what would you want to do?
- What is your favourite joke?
- If you won a million pounds, what would you do with it?
- Describe something you like about yourself.
- What is your favourite packed lunch?

Ask...

Why is it important to tell the truth? Can you think of situations when it would be really important?

> **Examples:** when a parent or teacher asks us for an answer.

Note: explain that sometimes it's OK to keep a secret, but only when it's a good secret, like a surprise party or birthday treat for someone.

Discuss...

How can we make sure we tell the truth all the time?

What the Bible says: Luke 9:18–20

Story: Jesus asks for the truth

One day Jesus was with his friends. Everyone knew about Jesus by now, but Jesus was curious to know what his friends thought about him. So he asked, 'Who do the crowds of people say I am?' They answered him truthfully: 'Some of them say you are a famous person from the past.'

He continued to ask. 'But you,' he said, 'who do you think I am?' One of Jesus' best friends, a man called Peter, said to him, 'I think you are the Son of God.' Jesus was very pleased with Peter's answer. He knew that Peter had said the truth.

What can we learn from the story?

What Peter said was a big statement. He was saying that Jesus was unique—a very special person, sent by God, to help people. But Peter knew it was the truth and wasn't afraid to say it, even if it was different from what people around him thought.

Reflection

It's important for us to make up our own minds sometimes—to find out the truth and then stick to it, no matter what anyone else says.

Uniqueness

Starter activity: Origami

First, fold a square piece of paper in half and half again. Press down to make clear creases, and unfold the paper. Fold the four corners in to the centre. Turn the paper over and fold the four corners in to the centre. Fold the paper in half. Slip a finger and thumb carefully under the square corner flaps. You can now open and close the shape in two different directions.

On the triangular inside flaps, write 'bird', 'animal', 'reptile' and 'insect'. You'll need to write each word twice, so that they can all be seen when the shape is opened in both directions. Then, underneath these flaps, write 'owl' (under 'bird'), 'monkey' (under 'animal'), 'snake' (under 'reptile' and 'bee' (under 'insect').

In pairs, one person chooses a number from 1 to 4. The other person opens and closes the shape that number of times. Choose an inside flap and act out the creature found under the flap.

Ask...

How many different birds, animals, reptiles and insects can you think of? What makes them unique or special? (You may need to explain that 'unique' means 'the only one of a kind'.)

> **Examples:** owls fly at night, hoot and can turn their heads right round; monkeys eat bananas and can swing from trees; snakes slither on the ground and can make their bodies into an 's' shape; bees buzz, make honey and tell other bees where flowers are by doing a special dance.

Discuss...

Everything has something unique about it—even people. What makes people in the group unique?

> **Examples:** Dom is good at football and is kind; Josh is funny and tells good jokes; Amy is creative and can draw well; Rosie loves singing and dancing.

What the Bible says: John 6:16–21

Story: Jesus walks on the water

Jesus' friends were in a boat on a lake. It was night. Suddenly, there was a big storm on the lake. There were very big waves and a strong wind. The boat started rocking from side to side. Even though Jesus' friends had been in a boat before, they were very scared. Then they saw something in the distance. It looked like a person—walking on the water. It couldn't be, could it? Yes, it was Jesus! Jesus' friends were amazed. Jesus was walking on the lake!

What can we learn from the story?

The Bible says that Jesus was the Son of God, which meant that Jesus could do very special things, such as raising people from the dead, healing people who were ill, and walking on a lake. Sometimes Jesus did really amazing things—so amazing that even his friends were astonished. Jesus wanted his friends to know that he could do amazing and good things for them.

Reflection

Everyone has special abilities, and sometimes those things can be surprising, too. We can all express and use our unique abilities.

Watching

Starter activity: Cartoon clip

Split the class into small groups and explain that you're going to play a clip from a cartoon. Ask the children to pay attention when they're watching it, because you're going to ask questions about it afterwards. Have a list of simple pre-prepared questions, such as 'What was so-and-so wearing?', 'How many animals were there?' and 'Where did the action take place?' The winning team is the one that gets the most answers right.

Ask...

What kinds of people have special jobs watching people, and why?

> **Examples:** spies, police, doctors and even teachers; to gather information; to catch criminals; to help make people better; to keep children safe and make sure they're learning the right things.

Discuss...

Why is it important to watch what's going on? What would happen if you didn't watch?

> **Examples:** to learn important things; to find out about new ideas; to test things and learn about the world around you; to learn how to do something new.

What the Bible says: Joshua 2:1–15

Story: Joshua sends spies into Jericho

Joshua sent two spies from his army into a city called Jericho. God had told Joshua to take the city for the Israelites, and Joshua wanted to find out more about Jericho. The two spies managed to get into the city, but news of them reached the king of Jericho. The king sent men out to try to find them, but the two spies were hiding at the house of a woman called Rahab. On her roof, drying in the sun, she had piles of flax—a type of plant from which people made linen for clothes. Rahab hid the spies under the flax on her roof.

After dark, she went to the spies. She said, 'We all know God is going to give our land to you, and all the people are afraid. I have been kind to you. I have hidden you from the king of Jericho. Please be kind to me when you come to take the city.' The spies promised that they would be kind—and they were. They also learned a lot from Rahab about the land and the people.

What can we learn from the story?

Even though God had told Joshua that Jericho would be a city for the Israelites to live in, Joshua needed more information. That's why he sent spies to find out more. He knew that the more information he had, the more successful he and his army would be.

Reflection

Sometimes, the more information we have, the more successful we are likely to be. If we watch carefully and ask good questions, we can find out more about what we need to do.

Working together

Starter activity: Pass it on

Divide the class into teams. Give them a selection of clothes, but make sure that no single group has a complete set. The aim is that the group must get one of their members dressed from head to toe with each of the following items: hat, glasses, scarf, coat, gloves, belt and thick socks.

Explain that the children are allowed to swap items with other groups, but they must ask politely and must always swap another item in return. Play until every group has a correctly dressed member.

Ask...

What does it feel like to share together? Is it easy or hard? What is it like when we ask for something we need and someone gives it to us?

> **Examples:** feels good; makes me happy; it's fun; we are more successful; it's more caring; gives me a warm feeling.

Discuss...

How can we be caring and sharing together?

> **Examples:** being quiet when the teacher is talking; waiting for lunch politely.

When you have discussed ways of caring and sharing, decide on an area of behaviour that you would like the class to work on together. Explain that this will be your aim for the next week or month. Discuss a suitable reward if you all manage to achieve the aim—perhaps bringing a special toy into school, having a pyjama day, playing games in the park, building a class den, singing songs, going for a picnic, or watching a DVD. Create a chart so that you can track your progress day by day.

What the Bible says: Matthew 25:31–40

Story: God likes people to work together

Jesus said that God likes people to care and share. He gives rewards to people for the good things they have done with each other and for each other. For example, God is happy when we give food to people who are hungry, water to people who are thirsty or clothes to people who need them. He likes it when we visit people who are ill or lonely or when we are kind to others, even if they're not popular or our best friends.

What can we learn from the story?

Christians believe that God likes people to care for each other, to share with each other and to make the world a better place. God likes it when we are kind and caring to ourselves and to each other and when we share what we have with others.

Reflection

Caring and sharing together makes us all feel happy and warm—a bit like some of the class felt when they were dressed in all those extra clothes.

 Reproduced with permission from *RE in the Classroom with 4–5s* by Helen Jaeger (Barnabas in Schools, 2015) www.barnabasinschools.org.uk

Outline for a themed day or assembly

Have a sleepy day with Sleepy Sloth

Here are some ideas for a day focused on rest and sleep. You could start with the story of Sleepy Sloth. It is shown below as a drama script with actions, in case you want to make a class play or assembly out of it. The whole class could repeat the refrain 'Go to bed, sleepy Sloth! Go to bed, sleepy head!' You could make masks for each of the other animals, and a sun and moon, too.

Sleepy Sloth doesn't want to go to bed. He thinks up lots of excuses to stay up past his bedtime. But if he doesn't go to sleep, he might not enjoy the next day, because he will be too tired. Can you help him go to sleep?

The scene is a rainforest with sun setting and moon rising.

Narrator: This is sleepy Sloth. He's very tired. He's so tired, he fell asleep…

Sloth looks exhausted as he arrives home from school and puts his bag down—with big dark rings around his eyes.

Narrator: … at school today… while watching television… when playing with friends… and eating his tea!

Sloth acts out each of these points.

Narrator: Now it's time for sleepy Sloth to go to bed. But sleepy Sloth says he *isn't* a sleepy head!

Climbs up towards his bed in the leaves of a tree, wearing stripy pyjamas, but looking reluctant to go to sleep.

Narrator: Will *you* help him go to sleep? Come on, sleepy Sloth! Up we go and into bed!

Sloth starts climbing again.

Narrator: Are you cosy in your bed? Sleep well, sleepy Sloth! Sleep well, sleepy head!

Sleepy Sloth is cosy in his bed, wrapped in a nice duvet in the leaves of the tree. Mummy Sloth gives him a big kiss goodnight.

Narrator: But sleepy Sloth doesn't want to sleep! Uh-oh. Here he is again.

Sloth peeks out from the leaves of the tree where his bed is. Mummy Sloth is watching television in dim light under the tree.

Narrator: 'Can I have a glass of water?' asks sleepy Sloth.

Sloth holds out empty cup and looks pleading.

Parrot / All: Go to bed, sleepy Sloth! Go to bed, sleepy head!

Narrator: 'But it's too quiet,' says sleepy Sloth.

Sloth is out of bed! He holds out his hands pleadingly.

Iguana / All: Go to bed, sleepy Sloth! Go to bed, sleepy head!

Narrator:	'Did I hear a noise?' asks sleepy Sloth.

Sloth is looking, or pretending to be, worried.

Orang-utan / All:	Go to bed, sleepy Sloth! Go to bed, sleepy head!
Narrator:	'But I'm lonely…' begins sleepy Sloth.

Sloth looks forlorn standing in his pyjamas, perhaps twisting a foot round and pleading.

Flying bat / All:	Go to bed, sleepy Sloth! Go to bed, sleepy head!
Narrator:	'What are you doing?' asks sleepy Sloth.

Sloth tries to engage in conversation with a monkey on a nearby tree.

Monkey / All:	Go to bed, sleepy Sloth! Go to bed, sleepy head!
Narrator:	'It's very hot,' says sleepy Sloth.

Sloth pulls at his pyjamas in a mock over-heating manoeuvre.

Tree frog / All:	Go to bed, sleepy Sloth! Go to bed, sleepy head!
Narrator:	'I'm feeling cold now,' says sleepy Sloth.

Sloth pretends to shiver and pulls pyjamas closer around him.

Toucan / All:	Go to bed, sleepy Sloth! Go to bed, sleepy head!
Narrator:	'Can I have a story?' asks sleepy Sloth.

Sloth holds out a book to read.

Jaguar / All:	Go to bed, sleepy Sloth! Go to bed, sleepy head!
Narrator:	Finally, sleepy Sloth falls asleep. Phew, at last! He's peacefully dreaming in his cosy bed.

Sloth is finally asleep, a glass of water and discarded book nearby. Sloth may even be snoring: he is definitely fast asleep.

Narrator:	Night night, sleepy Sloth! Night night, sleepy head! … Now, what about *you*?!

Other animals could be looking out of the rainforest all together at the same time.

Taking it further

You could do the following extension activities:

- Do some artwork with a South American rainforest theme or look at Aztec-style patterns.
- Have a pyjama day and allow the children to come in their pyjamas and dressing gowns, with their favourite teddy bear and story book.
- Play sleeping dogs (see page 47).
- Research five facts about sloths.
- Have a den building and reading time.
- Make 'sleepy' snacks, such as milk and bananas.
- Create your own rainforest, with painted leaves and flowers.
- Play gentle music and encourage the children to rest.
- Make box beds for their teddy bears and dolls, complete with bed coverings.
- Research facts about the benefits of sleep.
- Play 'Goodnight, Ben'. Ask the children to close their eyes and rest their heads on their hands (no peeking). Walk around the classroom tapping each child on the shoulder; the child must remember the name of the person who spoke before them and say 'Goodnight (name)' in order.
- Highlight and discuss a wildlife charity that supports animals such as the sloth.

Index of activities

About the author

Helen Jaeger is a writer, consultant, journalist and professional creative project manager with a background in teaching.

Enjoyed
this book?

Write a review—we'd love to hear what you think. Email: reviews@brf.org.uk

Keep up to date—receive details of our new books as they happen.
Sign up for email news and select your interest groups at:
www.brfonline.org.uk/findoutmore/

Follow us on Twitter @brfonline

By post—to receive new title information by post (UK only), complete the form below and post to: BRF Mailing Lists, 15 The Chambers, Vineyard, Abingdon, Oxfordshire, OX14 3FE

Your Details
Name _____
Address_____
_____
Town/City _____ Post Code _____
Email _____

Your Interest Groups (*Please tick as appropriate)

☐ Advent/Lent   ☐ Messy Church

☐ Bible Reading & Study   ☐ Pastoral

☐ Children's Books   ☐ Prayer & Spirituality

☐ Discipleship   ☐ Resources for Children's Church

☐ Leadership   ☐ Resources for Schools

Support your local bookshop
Ask about their new title information schemes.

Bottesford CE Primary School

Silverwood Road
Bottesford
Nottingham
NG13 0BS

Telephone - 01949 842224
Email - school@bottesford.leics.sch.uk
Website - www.bottesford.leics.sch.uk